How to Be a BAD Boyfriend

How to Be a BAD Boyfriend

The Girlfriends

iUniverse, Inc.
Bloomington

How to Be a BAD Boyfriend

iUniverse books may be ordered through booksellers or by contacting:

iUniverse
1663 Liberty Drive
Bloomington, IN 47403
www.iuniverse.com
1-800-Authors (1-800-288-4677)

ISBN: 978-1-4502-6989-6 (sc)
ISBN: 978-1-4502-6990-2 (e)

Printed in the United States of America

iUniverse rev. date: 08/05/2011

To all the Bad Boyfriends we dated,
who made this book possible.

PREFACE

With our combined years of dating, we felt a need to laugh out loud. A simple discussion about relationships between two friends turned into a humorous, six-hour road trip that will never be forgotten. We knew we needed to share our insights and put a positive spin on some less than appropriate behaviors. Thus, *How to Be a BAD Boyfriend* was launched.

Relating these experiences made us realize that there are other girlfriends out there who will also find our stories funny and perhaps will be able to laugh as they see their own situations unfolding. If you have a story that you would like to share, check out the form at the end of this book to submit your own Bad Boyfriend experience. If The Girlfriends decide it is appropriate for the next book, you will see it in *How to Be a BAD Boyfriend Part II.*

INTRODUCTION

When you're lying awake in bed or waiting in line at the checkout, do your thoughts take you to your last relationship? Are you feeling burned by someone who once had your heart? Have you ever wondered how others have learned to cope? So have we. Thus, as you read through these pages, more than likely you will laugh at our incidents and find the humor in your own situation as we bring the truth to light. For no experience, no matter how negative, should ever consume your precious life! If you can find humor in our experiences and laugh out loud, soon you will discover that your instances of remote viewing are nothing more than the Universe reminding you of something you do not want.

How to Be a BAD Boyfriend ...

1. Periodically make up a phone number, write it on a torn piece of paper, and put it in your pants pocket. Your girlfriend will find it when she does the laundry and know she'd better "shape up."

2. Talk incessantly about other girls. That way she'll know there is a lot of competition around.

I was just helping her out!

3. Don't call her when you are out of town. Keep her guessing what you're up to.

4. Have a one-night stand whenever you can. That will keep an edge on your prowess.

5. Have friendships with past girlfriends, especially those you slept with. Exclude your current girlfriend from participating in these relationships or even knowing they still exist.

6. Never insist on paying when she offers to pay.

7. Be a "womanizer."

8. Never offer to help carry in the groceries for your girlfriend. After all, she does need the exercise.

9. Ask her to marry you, but never set a date. This will ensure a free pass for sex.

10. Forget her birthday and then blame her because she didn't remind you.

11. Constantly criticize how she looks, how she acts, and her friends. She will appreciate your concern.

12. Have a parent/child relationship with you being the parent and her the child. That entitles you to tell her what to do.

13. Make sure you help ex-wives and girlfriends as soon as they call, making you the "good guy."

14. Fart in bed every chance you get.

15. Tell your girlfriend she is exactly like your ex-wife.

16. Buy souvenirs for other girls when you are on vacation with her.

17. Take other girls' calls when you are with her. After all, their time is

precious, and you don't want to miss any opportunities.

18. Make sure your mother and children from a previous relationship have a say about your current relationship.

19. Don't cut your hair or shave. Look slovenly, like a slob, when you see her.

I never promised that!

20. Shave your private parts when you know it repulses her.

21. If you are younger than she is, constantly remind her of this so she knows how lucky she is to have a young stud like you.

22. Take her home after a date, so you can go out with your friends.

23. Criticize her cooking; after all, it's not as good as your mother's.

24. Tell her she's fat.

25. Don't brush your teeth or bathe.

26. Continue to celebrate holidays and birthdays with your ex-in-laws and leave her home. Let her know she's not welcome there.

27. Walk ahead of her, so she is forced to follow you. It shows you are in charge.

28. Tell her you are far more advanced sexually than she is.

29. Refuse to introduce her to your family and friends. Likewise, don't meet hers.

30. Constantly blame her for everything that goes wrong in your life.

31. Don't include her in your kids' social events; just go by yourself.

32. Always be secretive. It will drive her crazy.

33. Check her caller ID. That way you can keep track of whom she talks to and how often.

34. When you're running late, don't bother calling to let her know.

35. Always interrupt her because, of course, your ideas are better.

36. Introduce her only as a "friend."

37. Get angry and pout, but don't discuss why.

38. Check her e-mail regularly.

39. Don't spring for a hotel or take her to your place for sex. Just do it in the car in the bar's parking lot. That way you can go for a nightcap alone when you're done.

40. Always put her down in front of friends, making her look inadequate.

41. Expect her to clean if she wants a clean house, because you are fine with it the way it is.

42. On a sub-zero night, sit in your warm truck with the heater on and watch her scrape ice off her new car to be sure she does it right. You are so thoughtful.

43. Keep the remote, because it's hard for her to make decisions.

You're driving me crazy!

44. Continuously check Internet dating sites to make sure you have the right girl.

45. Tell her she looks old so she will improve herself, making her look better on your arm. After all, your image is important.

46. Send flowers to your ex-mother-in-law—but not to your girlfriend—on her birthday and Mother's Day.

47. Always look at your waitress' breasts to avoid eye contact, because you wouldn't want to appear interested in front of your girlfriend.

48. Chew ravenously and with your mouth open whenever she cooks for you. Then she knows you appreciate it.

She's only a friend!

49. Flirt with other girls when you are with your girlfriend.

50. When she asks you to do something, pretend you didn't hear her. Then you can't be blamed when it's not done.

51. When you don't understand something she said, don't ask

for clarification. That's a sign of weakness.

52. Never open doors for her.

53. Ensure that she presoaks your T-shirts and underwear like your mother did.

54. Surprise her and come home with a new broom to make her life easier.

55. Always be evasive. That way you won't get into trouble.

You never listen!

56. Remember, omission is not betrayal or a lie.

57. If an argument starts, stop it in its tracks by saying, "I'm not going to discuss that with you." Hopefully it will be forgotten.

58. Remember, you are KING.

59. Tell her, "Do as I say, not as I do."

60. Always say, "I don't know" when she asks you to go somewhere you don't

want to go. That will appease her for awhile.

61. Make your girlfriend constantly chase you by always dangling that elusive "carrot," to make her work harder to please you.

62. Remember to give her just enough to keep her from running away, but never more.

You're always trying to change me!

63. Shave, use cologne, and dress attractively—then leave, so she wonders what you're up to.

64. Let her know that you are a gypsy at heart.

65. Tell her you're broke, so she doesn't expect to be taken out.

66. Constantly remind her that demanding girls are scum, so she is cautious not to be like that.

67. Be sure she knows how good she has it and that she is so lucky to have you.

68. Remind her that love is having sex daily.

69. Never take her to your favorite bar. Then you have an escape place she can't find.

It's not up for discussion!

70. Don't answer your cell phone when you know it's her calling.

71. When she leaves a message on your voice mail, don't call her until the next day.

72. Rub it in every time she's wrong.

73. Always bring up past disagreements for ammo. That way the current

issue gets lost and won't be discussed.

74. Have a stranger hit on your girlfriend to see if she will be faithful.

75. Never show your true feelings.

76. In the heat of passion, scream out an ex-girlfriend's name. Then reassure her she's the only one.

77. Never make plans more than three months out.

So what if I look!

78. Have a backup girlfriend waiting in the wings. It will keep you from getting too involved.

79. Make sure she knows that your friends and family always come first.

80. Offer to take her shopping for her Christmas gift the day after Christmas. The sales are good then, and after all, you like to save money.

81. To keep her hooked into you, subtly drop hints that you will get married, like browsing through bridal magazines with her. The fact you are a "confirmed bachelor" doesn't have to come up.

82. When the waiter asks for your order while dining out, always order first. It shows your importance.

83. When someone is talking to both of you and asks for an opinion, always assume they are asking for yours because you are smarter.

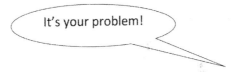

It's your problem!

84. When someone offers you a tray of food, always take yours first.

85. Get her drunk, so you can have your way with her.

86. When she asks for your "opinion," give her your "decision," and get angry when she doesn't do what you decided.

87. When your dog has an accident, make your girlfriend clean it up.

88. Fix yourself a late-night snack and never inquire whether she wants anything.

89. Throw out her favorite flannel nightgown, because it's not sexy enough for you.

90. Take your girlfriend to look at diamond rings. Then, when you know what she likes, buy her a fake one in the same design. Even though you are extremely frugal, you still are so good to her.

You don't trust me!

91. Don't groom yourself just to please her.

92. Attend friends' and co-workers' doings by yourself, because she won't know anyone. Just leave her home alone.

93. Ask her if she ever considered breast enhancements.

94. Keep a change of dress clothes in your car.

95. Spend late nights working on a project at a female co-worker's house, but don't tell your girlfriend. Then, when you come home and she asks where you were, just tell her "working." She just wouldn't understand.

It's all your fault!

96. When you don't call her back, tell her you lost your cell phone and don't know her number because it's programmed in your lost phone.

97. When your adult children don't like your girlfriend, make sure you spend time with them and their significant others, but leave your girlfriend at home. Then your children will

be happy that you respected their wishes.

98. When your adult children send nasty e-mails to your girlfriend, don't reprimand them. Just tell her that someday they'll come around.

99. Tell her your adult children do not need to respect her.

100. If you're in AA, make sure your sponsor is a member of the opposite sex.

It was just lunch!

101. Take her to dimly lit places, so no one can see who you're with.

102. Tell her you'll pick her up for a date after you eat dinner.

103. Make up lies as to where you've been, so you don't hurt her feelings. She is so sensitive.

104. Tell her you'll pick her up to go out; then fall asleep and don't show up.

105. Never ask her why she is crying.

106. Just stop calling her; you don't need to explain why.

107. If your mother doesn't like your girlfriend, assume there must be something wrong with her, because "Mother knows best."

108. Don't tell family and friends you are in a relationship.

109. Look at other girls when you're out on a date.

110. When someone misconstrues something your girlfriend did, never set them straight. Just let them believe the bad things are true, because you don't want to make waves.

111. Put your ex-in-laws' feelings above your girlfriend's, because they might die soon.

112. When it comes to another girl's advances toward you, tell your girlfriend she is not flirting with you; she's just being nice. It must be her insecurities and imagination overworking once again.

113. Respond to her bad mood with "What the @!?*%!."

Get over it!

114. Tell your girlfriend, "I'm tired of your bullshit."

115. Comment on your sex life to anyone who will listen.

116. Tell her, "It's all in your head. What have you been smoking?"

117. Do not appreciate the 101 things she does for you every week.

118. Take her for granted.

119. Always think something better is just around the corner.

120. Say to her, "Why can't you just listen?"

121. Be sure to have the last word.

122. Forget to show that you care.

123. Pick a fight in order to go out with your friends that night.

124. Take her out to eat and forget your wallet on a regular basis.

125. Always put her wishes last; yours come first.

126. Let her know that her ideas are always stupid and will never work.

127. Stay with her because you like hanging around her family and friends.

128. Never admit you're wrong.

129. Reminisce about all the good times with past girlfriends.

130. When you come home and she asks where you've been, reply, "Don't you trust me?" Then, never answer her question.

131. Pretend to be sick, so you don't have to go to her family function.

132. When you can't keep your erection, blame it on her.

If you loved me, you'd _____!

133. Post naked pictures of your girlfriend on the Internet.

134. Lie about your past.

135. Don't tell her you are married until several months into your relationship.

136. Sleep with her best friend.

137. Open the door so her cat runs away.

138. Purposely screw up the laundry so she yells at you. Then you can say, "Fine, I'll never do the laundry again."

139. Never apologize. That's a sign of weakness.

140. Volunteer her time for babysitting, baking, and running errands without checking with her. Then, when she can't do it, she'll be the "bad guy."

She's not flirting; she's just being nice!

141. Only go to your type of movie; it's "my movie or no movie."

142. Do last-minute shopping for her at the bewitching hour; just grab anything off the rack to be wrapped, even if it's two sizes too big.

143. Use her credit card.

144. At a dance, totally ignore her as you visit with all your friends.

145. When she tries to talk to you, put her on the defensive by saying, "You're always trying to change me."

146. Tell her she's acting crazy and it must be from too much caffeine. Then show her the decaffeinated coffee and cola you just bought her because you are so concerned.

When did I say that!

147. Leave the house by yourself or with friends and don't tell her where you're going.

148. Use cute pet names that she doesn't like.

149. Start a relationship with the girlfriend she invited to join the two of you for dinner. After all, it's always good to have a backup plan.

150. Take her to a dance but say you are going to dance with her sexy friend. When she replies, "As long as it's not the first or last dance," you say, "Any one she wants!"

151. Tell her that her lovemaking is the laziest ever.

152. Constantly point out her flaws when you are in a group of people.

153. Keep looking at all the sexily clad girls, and when she comments about it, tell her you're just looking for what would look cute on her.

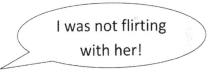

154. If she asks you what color her eyes are, tell her "brown," even though you know she has "baby blues."

155. Take her to dinner and tell her she can order anything she wants. Then ask the waiter for an extra plate so you can get your half.

156.   Install a listening device in her phone so you always know whom she is talking to and what about.

157.   Put liquor in your pop can so she never knows you're drinking.

158.   Remind her that guys and girls can never be friends because they will end up sleeping together; but that rule does not apply to you.

You're too sensitive!

159.   When the girl that is always flirting with you arrives late to the party, jump up and get her a chair next to you and your girlfriend, even though someone else has already provided one at the end of the table for her. The flirting will be good for your ego.

160.   Tell her you will never be in a relationship where you have to talk about issues.

161. Cancel your date with her at the last minute if a better opportunity presents itself.

162. The girl that always flirts with you in front of your girlfriend has a pair of concert tickets and asks you to go. When your steady girl doesn't think you should go, get very angry at her and pout and withhold affection for weeks.

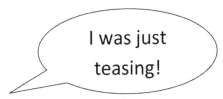

I was just teasing!

163. Set her up by constantly telling her all the cute things other girls are saying to you. Then get upset and yell if she becomes jealous.

164. Buy your female instructor a case of her favorite beer, so you can drink it with her when her hubby is out of town and your girlfriend is home alone.

165. Don't let your girlfriend have friends; they might put ideas in her head and cause trouble for you.

166. If your girlfriend is a good cook, make sure you get leftovers. Then on a date with someone else, you can pretend that you cooked it for her.

167. Tell her she can't go to the Singles Club you belong to, because that's your place and those are your friends.

She made a pass at me first!

168. Tell her you haven't met the right girl to get married. That will give her the ultimate challenge to please you.

169. Insist she wear the same perfume your ex did, because it's an instant turn on for you.

170. Always be unaccountable; it's your "man" right.

171.   And lastly … show her …

No R E S P E C T !

Submission Form

If you would like to send in a short personal example of a "Bad Boyfriend," send to:

The Girlfriends
PO Box 75
Lomira, WI 53048

Experience: _____

_____

_____

_____

_____

_____

Submitted By: _____ (First Name)

_____ (City) _____ (State)

(Example: Sally from Dixon, IL)

Would you like your first name, city, and state listed under your experience in the next publication? Yes __ No __

Signature authorizing The Girlfriends to include your experience in the next book:

_____

_____

Thank You for Sharing ……..

The Girlfriends

One of the authors of this book started out as an executive assistant at a large corporation. Then she read a book that advised to make your passion your career, and you will always love it. That passion is interior design and she pursued the study of it. Using her education, she has a successful career in sales in the furniture industry, working with clients and advising them on their décor which she totally enjoys. She loves music and lives in Milwaukee, Wisconsin, home of "Summerfest", the largest outdoor music fest in the world, which she attends, often daily. She spends her time going to concerts, travelling, gardening and with family and friends.

♥   ♥   ♥

The other author lives and works out of her home located in rural Wisconsin. She earned a B.S. in Business Administration and a J.D. Although law and mediation are a passion she ended up founding a successful company that specializes in safety awareness for large and small corporations. Divorced twice, she has two grown children that live in California and enjoys travelling to visit with them and her first grandchild. Her first love is being one with nature; whether viewing mountain ranges, forests or prairie - just being outside is the main goal. She is also a Soroptomist sister and enjoys the camaraderie that comes with helping others.

❤   ❤   ❤

This book is written under the pen name "The Girlfriends". These friends have been together since 1989 and have shared many of life's experiences with each other. These include marriage, divorce, dating, boyfriends and new relationships. Their combined stories and dating experiences encouraged them to write this book as an awareness guide for girlfriends of all ages. They hope you will gain insight, laugh a little and enjoy their book.

♥   ♥   ♥

NOTES

NOTES

NOTES